SANTA ANA PUBLIC LIBRARY

AR PTS: 0.5

Superstars
of the
LOS ANGELES
DODGERS

By Max Hammer

amicus
high interest

Amicus High Interest is published by Amicus
P.O. Box 1329, Mankato, MN 56002
www.amicuspublishing.us

Library of Congress Cataloging-in-Publication Data
Hammer, Max.
  Superstars of the Los Angeles Dodgers / by Max Hammer.
      pages cm. -- (Pro sports superstars)
  Includes index.
  Summary: "Presents some of the Los Angeles Dodgers' greatest players
and their achievements in pro baseball, including Mike Piazza and
Clayton Kershaw"--Provided by publisher.
  ISBN 978-1-60753-593-5 (hardcover) -- ISBN 978-1-60753-627-7 (pdf
ebook)
  1. Los Angeles Dodgers (Baseball team)--History--Juvenile literature.
2. Baseball players--United States--History. I. Title.
  GV875.L6H35 2014
  796.357›640979494--dc23
                              2013048644

Photo Credits: Alex Gallardo/AP Images, cover; Lenny Ignelzi/AP Images,
2, 15; Zuma Press/Icon SMI, 5; Bettmann/Corbis, 7, 8, 11; Focus on Sport/
Getty Images, 12; Eric Risberg/AP Images, 16, 22; Chris Williams/Icon SMI,
19; Mark J. Terrill/AP Images, 21

Produced for Amicus by The Peterson Publishing Company
and Red Line Editorial.

Editor Arnold Ringstad
Designer Maggie Villaume
Printed in the United States of America
Mankato, MN
2-2014
PA10001
10 9 8 7 6 5 4 3 2 1

TABLE OF CONTENTS

MEET THE LOS ANGELES DODGERS

The Dodgers started in 1884. They first played in Brooklyn. The team moved to Los Angeles in 1958. The Dodgers have had many stars. Here are some of the best.

JACKIE ROBINSON

Jackie Robinson played for the Dodgers when they were in Brooklyn. In 1947 he became the first African-American major league player. Robinson was a great hitter and fielder. He played in six **World Series**.

Jackie Robinson's uniform number, 42, was retired in his honor.

8

SANDY KOUFAX

Sandy Koufax was a pitcher.
He had a great **fastball**. He threw
sharp **curveballs**. He won three
Cy Young Awards. The last was
in 1966.

Sandy Koufax played basketball
in college.

MAURY WILLS

Maury Wills played shortstop. He was a fast runner. His best year was in 1962. Wills stole 104 bases. He won a Most Valuable Player award that year.

STEVE GARVEY

Steve Garvey was a great first baseman. He first played in 1969. He missed no games between 1975 and 1983. That is a team record for games played in a row.

OREL HERSHISER

Orel Hershiser was a star pitcher.

He threw many kinds of pitches.

Some went fast and straight.

Others curved. His best season was

in 1988. He won a Cy Young Award.

In 1988 Hershiser pitched 59 innings in a row without giving up a run.

16

MIKE PIAZZA

Mike Piazza played catcher. He was also a strong hitter. Piazza won ten **Silver Slugger Awards**. He also hit many **home runs**. He hit 40 in 1997.

Mike Piazza has more home runs than any other catcher.

CLAYTON KERSHAW

Clayton Kershaw is a great pitcher. Teams score few runs against him. Kershaw won Cy Young Awards in 2011 and 2013.

Many writers have compared Kershaw to Sandy Koufax.

YASIEL PUIG

Yasiel Puig joined the Dodgers in 2013. He began playing in the middle of the season. Puig soon became a star for his strong hitting. He hit two home runs in his second game.

The Dodgers have had many great superstars. Who will be next?

TEAM FAST FACTS

Founded: 1884

Other names: Brooklyn Atlantics (1884), Brooklyn Grays (1885–1887), Brooklyn Bridegrooms (1888–1890, 1896–1898), Brooklyn Grooms (1891–1895), Brooklyn Superbas (1899–1910, 1913), Brooklyn Dodgers (1911–12, 1932–57), Brooklyn Robins (1913–1931)

Nicknames: Los Doyers, The Blue Crew

Home Stadium: Dodger Stadium (Los Angeles, California)

World Series Championships: 6 (1955, 1959, 1963, 1965, 1981, 1988)

Hall of Fame Players: 46, including Sandy Koufax and Jackie Robinson (also nine managers)

WORDS TO KNOW

Cy Young Awards – awards given to the best pitcher in each league after each season

curveballs – pitches that spin and dive as they go forward

fastball – a pitch that goes fast and straight

home runs – hits that go far enough to leave the field, letting the hitter run all the way around the bases to score a run

Silver Slugger Awards – awards given to the best hitters each year

World Series – the annual baseball championship series

LEARN MORE

Books

Kelley, K. C. *Los Angeles Dodgers (Favorite Baseball Teams)*. North Mankato, MN: The Child's World, 2010.

LeBoutillier, Nate. *The Story of the Los Angeles Dodgers*. Mankato, MN: Creative Education, 2012.

Web Sites

Baseball History
http://mlb.mlb.com/mlb/history
Learn more about the history of baseball.

Los Angeles Dodgers—Official Site
http://dodgers.mlb.com
Watch video clips and read stories about the Los Angeles Dodgers.

MLB.com
http://mlb.com
See pictures and track your favorite baseball player's stats.

INDEX